Measuring Success in

Maths

Y4

Mental and Written Tests for YEAR 4

Holy

Email: o
Web: w

...sch.uk

GL
assessment
the measure of potential

Jenny Lawson

GL assessment
the measure of potential

Published by GL Assessment Limited 2008
The Chiswick Centre, 414 Chiswick High Road, London W4 5TF

GL Assessment is part of the Granada Learning Group

Measuring Success in Maths: Year 4 copyright © Jenny Lawson 2008

ISBN 978 0 7087 1786 8

The right of Jenny Lawson to be identified as author of this work has been asserted by her in accordance with the Copyright, Designs and Patents Act, 1988.

All rights reserved, including translation. Except where otherwise indicated, no part of this publication may be reproduced or stored in any form or by any means, electronic or mechanical, including photocopying, recording or duplication in any information storage and retrieval system, without permission in writing from the publishers, and may not be photocopied or otherwise reproduced even within the terms of any licence granted by the Copyright Licensing Agency Ltd.

Photocopying restrictions
Photocopiable pages 14–70: The purchase of this copyright material confers the right on the purchasing institution to photocopy the pages for their own use or for their pupils' use within the purchasing institution. No other part of this publication may be reproduced or stored in any form or by any means, electronic or mechanical, including photocopying, recording or duplication in any information storage and retrieval system, without prior permission in writing from GL Assessment and may not be photocopied or otherwise reproduced even within the terms of the any licence granted by the Copyright Licensing Agency Ltd.

If you have any doubts about your use of the photocopiable material in this publication, please contact the permissions department at GL Assessment.

Series developed by Emma Rees
Concept design by Lorraine Inglis
Cover image: Laurence Monneret, Stone/Getty Images
Illustrations by Kim Blundell
Typeset by FiSH Books
Printed in Great Britain

Contents

● About the author

Jenny Lawson is an experienced teacher and examiner of Mathematics and ICT, with a long career in education and educational publishing. Jenny recently returned to the classroom, teaching in a specialist school environment with responsibility for those needing to overcome learning difficulties related to mathematical concepts. She is a much published author of Mathematics and ICT texts for all ages and all levels, from the least able to the most gifted.

● Acknowledgements

The author and publishers are grateful for the invaluable advice and feedback of the following people during the development of *Measuring Success in Maths*:

- Sue Brown, Teacher,
  Malden Parochial Church of England Primary School, Surrey

- Paul Collins, Deputy Headteacher and Numeracy Co-ordinator,
  Albert Elliott Primary School, South Tyneside

- Gail Howe, Deputy Headteacher,
  Wardley Primary School, Gateshead

- Helen Millburn, Year 1 Teacher and Pupil Improvement Co-ordinator,
  Toner Avenue Primary School, South Tyneside

- Rachel Scott, Key Stage 2 Co-ordinator,
  All Saints' Church of England Primary School, South Tyneside

Introduction

'Good teachers track the progress of their pupils closely and adjust their teaching to ensure that all make the best possible progress.'[1]

● The *Measuring Success* series

Measuring Success is a new series of photocopiable topic tests for Years 1 to 6. These tests will help you assess the growing understanding of your pupils quickly and effectively. Use them as pupils complete the relevant topics to:

- help identify their needs;
- inform your future teaching;
- provide evidence to support teacher assessment levels at the end of Key Stages 1 and 2.

QCA is encouraging teachers to carry out more regular formative – 'periodic' – testing, for which *Measuring Success* provides the ideal solution.

The *Measuring Success* tests have been written by subject specialists who are experienced authors, teachers and INSET providers. They have been developed and trialled in conjunction with a team of subject specialists and practitioners. The test content is informed by past national tests questions and by the longstanding expertise of GL Assessment, a specialist publisher in assessment. The first titles in the series are for Maths and Science.

● *Measuring Success in Maths:* Overview

Measuring Success in Maths comprises differentiated Mental and Written Tests for Years 1 to 6, organised by the five blocks of work indicated in the renewed *Primary Framework for literacy and mathematics.*

Tasks are also included for Key Stage 1 in addition to these tests. The Key Stage 1 tasks and tests are presented in one book and Years 3 to 6 each in separate books.

The tasks and tests can also be used with other curricula not based around the *Primary Framework for literacy and mathematics.*

---

[1] *Making Good Progress* (DfES 2006)

Aims

The *Measuring Success in Maths* assessment activities will enable you to test the growing mathematical understanding of your pupils – both individually and as a group – quickly and efficiently. They offer an opportunity to plan your teaching – and so pupils' future learning – on their current understanding.

Used across the school, *Measuring Success in Maths* will provide a consistent ongoing approach to monitoring pupils' understanding and progress. Good monitoring ensures progression and the most effective use of teaching time.

Structure

The tests are structured according to pupils' age group and needs.

- Year I eases pupils into assessment. Term I comprises entirely Tasks. These encourage small group work and teacher observation, following the approach of the national tests. Term 2 introduces Mental Maths Tests, building up to Written Tests in Term 3. There are 15 Tasks, 10 Mental Maths Tests and 5 Written Tests in total, organised in the 5 Framework blocks.
- In Year 2 there are 3 Tasks, 3 Mental Maths Tests and 3 Written Tests for each block.
- In Years 3–6 there are 3 Mental Maths Tests and 3 Written Tests for each block.

The tests increase in difficulty across each block. They can be used progressively across the year, either one test per term for each block, or chosen according to pupil ability.

The tests in Blocks A and E focus on number and incorporate objectives from three strands:

- Counting and understanding number;
- Knowing and using number facts;
- Calculating.

The intermediate Blocks B, C and D focus on the other strands:

- Understanding shape (Blocks B and D);
- Measuring (Block C and D);
- Handling data (Block C).

Where two blocks cover similar material, the second one stretches pupils in some way. See Topic Coverage charts for an overview of the coverage.

Question types

The Mental Tests focus on questions that are best presented orally. The selection of questions for tests within a block is biased towards material that is relevant for that block. However, since not all topics lend themselves to oral testing, in some blocks (for example Blocks B and D) the Mental Tests may also include questions that relate to earlier blocks. Such questions thus provide a check on retention.

Each Mental Test has 15 questions, split into three sections for which 5, 10 and 15 seconds should be allowed per question.

- The **5-second** questions are straightforward and rely on recall of facts, number bonds and the times tables.
- The **10-second** questions require pupils to retain information.
- The **15-second** questions tax the pupils, with the need to retain more information and to perform a more complex calculation.

The three Written Tests in each block are provided at a range of levels and the questions increase in difficulty across each test. There are 8 questions in each of the Key Stage 1 Written Tests and 10 in each of the Key Stage 2 tests.

The questions in the Written Tests offer a variety of formats, for example, with pupils entering an answer into a box, circling a correct answer, matching activities and so on. As the questions rely on visual clues and/or require working out to be done, they would therefore not be suitable for oral delivery. Having completed a number of tests, some of the formats will become familiar and this should prepare pupils for answering different question types.

At Key Stage 1 the amount of text is limited, to reflect children's emerging literacy. This is supported by the use of repeated activity types and common instructions, to help familiarise pupils with the approach.

Calculators are not permitted for the tests except in Year 6. Where there is a requirement for pupils to demonstrate skills in using a calculator, this is achieved by asking questions about calculator usage. Calculators are allowed in all the Year 6 Written Tests and the questions involve more complex numbers.

When to use the tests

The tests are designed to allow maximum flexibility in their use.

- You may set a test before embarking on a block, to check what pupils already understand.
- You may set a test when you have completed material for a particular block to assess pupils' understanding of the topic and identify areas for further development.
- You may set a test later in the year for revision purposes.
- You might like to use the Mental Maths Tests first, as a 'warm up' for the Written Tests.

The tests can therefore be used at whatever point in the year that suits you, your class or individual pupils.

The results of these tests can be used to focus your teaching. They will highlight weaknesses – but remember (more importantly) that they will also highlight strengths – so celebrate the children's success!

Level coverage

The tests cover the following National Curriculum levels:

- Year 1   Levels 1–2
- Year 2   Levels 1–3
- Year 3   Levels 1–3
- Year 4   Levels 2–4
- Year 5   Levels 3–5
- Year 6   Levels 3–5

The tests increase in difficulty across each block. Where tests in a block share the same level, the proportion of questions at the higher level will be greater in the later tests. The difficulty of the topic is reflected where levels differ across blocks.

The breakdown of levels for the Written Tests is as follows:

KS2	Block A	Block B	Block C	Block D	Block E
Year 3					
Test 1	L1–3	L1–3	L1–3	L1–3	L2–3
Test 2	L2–3	L2–3	L2–3	L2–3	L2–3
Test 3	L2–3	L2–3	L2–3	L2–3	L2–3
Year 4					
Test 1	L3	L2–3	L2–4	L2–3	L3–4
Test 2	L3–4	L3–4	L3–4	L3–4	L3–4
Test 3	L3–4	L3–4	L3–4	L3–4	L3–4
Year 5					
Test 1	L3	L2–4	L3	L3–4	L3–4
Test 2	L3	L3–4	L3–4	L3–4	L4–5
Test 3	L3–4	L3–4	L4	L4	L4–5
Year 6					
Test 1	L3	L4	L3–5	L3–4	L3–4
Test 2	L4	L4	L4–5	L4	L3–5
Test 3	L4–5	L4–5	L4–5	L4–5	L4–5

⬤ Administering the tests

Tests need not be threatening. There is plenty of evidence that we all like a challenge to our knowledge and understanding, which accounts for the popularity of pub quizzes and crosswords. Approach the tests in this way. They are a challenge, not a chore.

When using the tests:

- Explain to the children that the test will enable them to show what they *have* learned, not catch them out over things they *haven't*. You could tell them quite freely, in advance, what areas they will be tested on. Reassure them that they will not be asked questions about mathematics they have not done.

- Explain that the questions are based on recent work and should be *familiar*. Remind pupils what you have been learning about, so they put the test in the right context. You don't want them to come out saying 'We didn't learn about that'.

- Show pupils *examples* of how to make choices – true/false, yes/no, ✓, circle and so on. Explain that they can go back and correct their answers if they later change their mind.

- For practical reasons, you will need to put a time limit on the tests. The Mental Maths Tests should take about 5–10 minutes each, depending on the speed of delivery and the time you allow pupils to answer the questions. The Written Tests should take approximately 20–30 minutes. In a single lesson, there should be time for a Mental and a Written Test if you wish.

- While you will need to make arrangements to prevent cheating – or you will not record accurate results – don't make a big deal of the tests by varying classroom routine too much.

- Remember that we all perform better when we are relaxed and confident. The tests aim to show pupils – and their learning – in the best possible light.

Marking the tests

Don't be anxious yourself. This is not an acid test of your teaching. However well you have taught something, there may still be some children who have difficulty with recall and with performance in 'test' conditions. This should not be a burden to them – or to you.

Please also bear in mind that the results represent pupils' performance in the particular test alone. This will complement your impression of their wider general performance. It is always best to consider test results in combination with everything else you know about a child. For example, you might realise that a child who has done surprisingly well on the test is typically withdrawn and timid in group activities, so that his or her level of knowledge and understanding could be underestimated. Another child might do surprisingly poorly on the test and that could prompt you to recognise that they are better at oral activities or do better when there is social support and feedback from other people.

In the final analysis – trust your own judgement. Some children find it difficult to shine in any assessment; others may just be having a bad day. This is a resource to enhance, not inhibit, your teaching of mathematics.

Allocating and recording marks

The questions are easy to **mark**:

- The Mental Maths Test marking could be done in class, with the pupils swapping answer sheets and marking each other's as you read aloud both the question and its answer. You could then elaborate on any questions for which the majority of pupils gave the wrong answer. You could also follow up with individuals who are having specific problems.

- Most Written Test questions have a single answer, or a choice from very few, correct answers.

- A standard approach to scoring has been used throughout, with 1 point generally allocated to each separate part of the question asked.

Score box

- The score box to the right of the question indicates the total number of points available for the question. It includes a space to record the mark awarded.

- Use the **Class Record Sheets** at the end of the book to record the raw scores for each pupil in the Mental and Written Tests. These will build up to provide an overview of class performance across the year. (You can photocopy these to add an extra sheet, according to the size of your class.)

Level interpretation

- The Mental Maths Tests will give you an impression of a child's performance, which builds up into a more detailed picture through the Written Tests, for which indicative National Curriculum levels are provided. In order to equate your pupils' performance in the Written Tests to National Curriculum levels, we have provided a **Level Converter**. Simply enter pupils' raw scores for a Written Test into the spreadsheet and it will calculate an indicative National Curriculum level. Once pupils have completed all the Written Tests, it will calculate a level for overall performance across the year, based on the performance data.

- The Level Converter will also calculate the number of pupils working at or towards the relevant National Curriculum levels covered by each test.

- The level interpretation is based on an analysis of the number of points allocated to each National Curriculum level in a test. The level of each question has been informed by specialist expertise and coverage of the relevant QCA objectives. Pupils' success in questions at different levels determines the indicative National Curriculum level which they are at or working towards. To achieve a level, a pupil must get the majority of the available marks at that level.

- The statistical formula we have used to calculate the levels draws on the longstanding expertise of GL Assessment gained in developing the leading high stakes standardised assessments that many of you use.

- Bear in mind that the levels suggested are purely indicative and, apart from the overall level, represent performance in a single Written Test focused on a specific topic. They serve to highlight pupils' skills and understanding in a discrete topic. As pupils complete more Written Tests, you will build up a cumulative impression of the relative strength or weakness between different topics.

- The cumulative data gained will give you a more accurate judgment of the pupil's overall level in mathematics. The levels should be used to complement pupils' scores in the Mental Maths Tests and teachers' own impression of a pupil's performance, rather than be used in isolation to form the basis for judging a pupil's overall skills and understanding in mathematics.

- To access the Level Converter, go to: **www.measuringsuccessonline.com/maths** and follow the instructions.

Sublevels

- It would take a much longer test, and a great many more questions, to establish sublevels of children's performance. If you are asked to provide sublevels, you may use your professional judgement based on the results of these tests and children's other work in mathematics.

- Combining your knowledge of the children with test results will enable you to plan more effectively. It may lead you to setting and grouping the children, but all your decisions should put their learning first. Secure evaluation will lead to sound teaching and learning.

Evaluating performance

The *Measuring Success* series can help in many different areas associated with evaluating performance, contributing to your identifying pupils who need support and those who may be Gifted and Talented, for example.

- The different types of test will help identify pupils' relative strengths and weaknesses in these different skills.

- As each Mental Maths Test is broken down into three sections of increasing difficulty, look at pupils' scores for each section to identify any problems they may have, reviewing performance across the class.

- As the tests across a block increase in difficulty, you can quickly see where a child's understanding is limited and where some remedial work will be needed.

- The tests will offer you an overview of the progress of the whole group.

- They will help you record children performing well in the tests as at or close to the expected level for that area of work.

- You can recognise those children who have scored higher as above the average test level and note that they may need stretching in future.

- You can recognise those children who have low scores and need support. You can recognise, as the wrong answers pile up, those who may have resorted to guessing.

Developing the *Measuring Success* series

These tests were developed in partnership with teachers – and your feedback on using the tests will help us develop and refine the series further. The tests and the accompanying National Curriculum level interpretation will be reviewed, when required, in response to changes in national standards and an analysis of pupil performance in the tests. If you would like to contribute to the development of this series by helping us collect pupil performance data and/or becoming involved in future trialling of material, please email the publisher at: measuringsuccess@gl-assessment.co.uk.

For further information about the *Measuring Success* series and sample material from other titles in the series, go to: **www.gl-assessment.co.uk/measuringsuccess**.

Topic Coverage – Year 4

	A	B	C	D	E
Using and applying mathematics					
Solve one- and two-step problems involving numbers, money or measures, including time; choose and carry out appropriate calculations, using calculator methods where appropriate	✓	✓		✓	
Represent a puzzle or problem using number sentences, statements or diagrams; use these to solve the problem; present and interpret the solution in the context of the problem					✓✓
Suggest a line of enquiry and the strategy needed to follow it; collect, organise and interpret selected information to find answers			✓✓		
Identify and use patterns, relationships and properties of numbers or shapes; investigate a statement involving numbers and test it with examples		✓✓			
Report solutions to puzzles and problems, giving explanations and reasoning orally and in writing, using diagrams and symbols	✓	✓	✓		
Counting and understanding number					
Recognise and continue number sequences formed by counting on or back in steps of constant size	✓✓				
Partition, round and order four-digit whole numbers; use positive and negative numbers in context and position them on a number line; state inequalities using the symbols < and >	✓✓				
Use decimal notation for tenths and hundredths and partition decimals; relate the notation to money and measurement; position one-place and two-place decimals on a number line	✓			✓	
Recognise the equivalence between decimal and fraction forms of one half, quarters, tenths and hundredths					✓✓
Use diagrams to identify equivalent fractions; interpret mixed numbers and position them on a number line					
Use the vocabulary of ratio and proportion to describe the relationship between two quantities, e.g. there are 2 red beads to every 3 blue beads; estimate a proportion, e.g. 'about one quarter of the apples in the box are green'					✓✓
Knowing and using number facts					
Use knowledge of addition and subtraction facts and place value to derive sums and differences of pairs of multiples of 10, 100 or 1000	✓	✓			
Identify the doubles of two-digit numbers; use to calculate doubles of multiples of 10 and 100 and derive the corresponding halves	✓	✓			
Derive and recall multiplication facts up to 10 x 10, the corresponding division facts and multiples of numbers to 10 up to the tenth multiple	✓	✓		✓	✓

 Extracts from *Primary Framework for literacy and mathematics* © Crown copyright 2006. Reproduced under the terms of the Click-Use Licence.

Objective	1	2	3	4	5
Use knowledge of rounding, number operations and inverses to estimate and check calculations	✓	✓			
Identify pairs of fractions that total 1					✓✓
Calculating					
Add or subtract mentally pairs of two-digit whole numbers	✓			✓	
Refine and use efficient written methods to add and subtract two- and three-digit whole numbers and £.p	✓			✓	
Multiply and divide numbers to 1000 by 10 and then 100 (whole-number answers), understanding the effect; relate to scaling up or down	✓✓				
Develop and use written methods to record, support and explain multiplication and division of two-digit numbers by a one-digit number, including division with remainders	✓			✓	✓
Find fractions of numbers, quantities or shapes					✓✓
Use a calculator to carry out one-step and two-step calculations involving all four operations; recognise negative numbers in the display, correct mistaken entries and interpret the display correctly in the context of money	✓✓				
Understanding shape					
Draw polygons and classify them by identifying their properties, including their line symmetry		✓✓			
Visualise 3-D objects from 2-D drawings; make nets of common solids		✓✓			
Recognise horizontal and vertical lines; use the eight compass points to describe direction; describe and identify the position of a square on a grid of squares				✓✓	
Know that angles are measured in degrees and that one whole turn is 360°; draw, compare and order angles less than 180°				✓✓	
Measuring					
Choose and use standard metric units and their abbreviations when estimating, measuring and recording length, weight and capacity; know the meaning of 'kilo', 'centi' and 'milli' and, where appropriate, use decimal notation to record measurements			✓	✓	
Interpret intervals and divisions on partially numbered scales; record readings accurately, to the nearest $\frac{1}{10}$ of a unit			✓	✓	
Draw rectangles + measure + calculate their perimeters; find the area of rectilinear shapes on a square grid by counting squares				✓✓	
Read time to the nearest minute; use am, pm and 12-hour clock notation; choose units of time to measure time intervals; calculate time intervals from clocks and timetables				✓✓	
Handling data					
Answer a question by identifying what data to collect; organise, present, analyse and interpret the data in tables, diagrams, tally charts, pictograms and bar charts, using ICT where appropriate			✓✓		
Compare the impact of representations where scales have intervals of differing step size			✓✓		

✓ indicates inclusion of objective in the Block; ✓✓ indicates that the tests focus on the objective.

Block A — Counting, partitioning and calculating

There are 15 questions in this test. Listen carefully to each question and then write down your answer.

5 seconds	**Answers**
① Write the number seven thousand and thirty-eight in figures.	7038
② Write the number that is five squared.	25
③ What is one-tenth as a decimal?	0.1
④ What is double seventeen?	34
⑤ What is half of twenty-eight?	14

10 seconds	
⑥ What are the next three numbers in this sequence: two, four, six, …?	8, 10, 12
⑦ Add twenty-nine and twenty-six.	55
⑧ Subtract thirteen from thirty.	17
⑨ What is ten times thirty-six?	360
⑩ What is one hundred times twenty-four?	2400

15 seconds	
⑪ How many months are there in two and a half years?	30
⑫ Fifty-four pupils go to a sports match by minibus. Each minibus carries eighteen passengers. How many minibuses are needed?	3
⑬ I am thinking of a number. I take away fifteen and get thirty-eight. What is my number?	53
⑭ I am thinking of a number between seventy and eighty. When I divide by ten, the remainder is four. What is my number?	74
⑮ The difference between two numbers is seventeen. The smaller number is forty-five. What is the other number?	62

Measuring Success in Maths: Year 4 © Jenny Lawson 2008. GL Assessment Limited

There are 15 questions in this test. Listen carefully to each question and then write down your answer.

5 seconds	**Answers**
(1) Write the number six thousand and twenty-two in figures.	6022
(2) What is seven squared?	49
(3) What is one-half as a decimal?	0.5
(4) What is half of twenty-two?	11
(5) How many hours are there in two days?	48

10 seconds	
(6) Add twenty-eight and twenty-seven.	55
(7) What is sixteen less than thirty-one?	15
(8) What is double nineteen?	38
(9) What is two thousand, one hundred divided by ten?	210
(10) What is one hundred times twenty-eight?	2800

15 seconds	
(11) What are the next three numbers in this sequence: one, three, five, …?	7, 9, 11
(12) Eight friends share equally a packet of twenty-four biscuits. How many biscuits does each person have?	3
(13) Add four and twenty-one and then divide the result by five.	5
(14) Two numbers have a difference of eight. The bigger number is twenty-one. What is the other number?	13
(15) A number lies between forty and fifty. When the number is divided by ten there is a remainder of seven. What is the number?	47

There are 15 questions in this test. Listen carefully to each question and then write down your answer.

5 seconds	**Answers**
(1) Write the number four thousand and nineteen in figures.	4019
(2) What is six times six?	36
(3) What is one-hundredth as a decimal?	0.01
(4) What is half of twenty-six?	13
(5) What is double eighteen?	36

10 seconds	
(6) Add twenty-four and twenty-seven.	51
(7) How many days are there in three weeks?	21
(8) What is three thousand three hundred divided by one hundred?	33
(9) What is ten times forty-six?	460
(10) What are the next three numbers in this sequence: three, six, nine, …?	12, 15, 18

15 seconds	
(11) What is the difference between thirty-two and seventeen?	15
(12) How many five-a-side teams can be made from a group of twenty-five people?	5
(13) Divide the sum of five and nineteen by three.	8
(14) The sum of two numbers is eighty-two. One of the numbers is twenty-one. What is the other one?	61
(15) A number lies between sixty and seventy. When the number is divided by ten there is a remainder of two. What is the number?	62

Mental Maths Test A___

Name _____

Write the answer to each question in the space provided.

5 seconds

1		
2		
3		
4		
5		

10 seconds

6		
7		
8		
9		
10		

15 seconds

11		
12		
13		
14		
15		

Mental Maths Test A___

Name _____

Write the answer to each question in the space provided.

5 seconds

1		
2		
3		
4		
5		

10 seconds

6		
7		
8		
9		
10		

15 seconds

11		
12		
13		
14		
15		

Name _____ Class _____ Date _____

1 What is the biggest 4-digit number you can create with these digits?

3   6   1   9

_____   ▢ 1

2 Jake and Mai are talking about numbers.

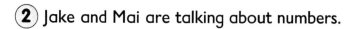

> 5 hundreds is less than 51 tens

Jake

> 5 hundreds is more than 51 tens

Mai

Who is right? _____   ▢ 1

3 Complete these sums.

a 100 + ☐ = 450   **b** 430 − ☐ = 200   ▢ 2

4 Complete these sums.

a 5 × 3 − 2 = ☐   **b** 24 ÷ 6 − 2 = ☐   ▢ 2

5 Choose a number to make these statements correct.

a ☐ + 13 < 20   **b** 20 > ☐ − 4   ▢ 2

6 Circle two sums that give the same answer.

3 × 5   6 × 2   3 × 6   4 × 4   9 × 2   ▢ 1

Measuring Success in Maths: Year 4 © Jenny Lawson 2008. GL Assessment Limited

⑦ A cinema brochure says it has 400 seats.
This is accurate to the nearest 100.

   a What is the least number of seats in the cinema? _____

   b What is the greatest number of seats in the cinema? _____ | 2 |

⑧ Jake made some mistakes in these multiplication sums.
What should his answers have been?

```
a   2   3          b   I   3
  x   4              x   6
  -------            -------
  8   0              6   0
      7              I   6
  -------            -------
  8   7              7   6
  -------            -------
```

   a _____

   b _____ | 2 |

⑨ Mai presses these keys on her calculator to work out a sum:

What will the calculator display show?

 | I |

⑩ Here is a diagram for sorting numbers.

	Even	Not even
less than 10	4, 6	5, 7
not less than 10	14, 18	15, 17

Put the numbers 1, 2, 12 and 19 in their correct places in the table. | I |

A2

Name _____ Class _____ Date _____

1 Complete these sums.

a [   ] − 430 = 200   **b** 99 + [   ] = 170   [2]

2 a What is the smallest 4-digit number you can create with these digits?

　　2　　7　　5　　1　　　　　　　　　　　_____

b What is the biggest 4-digit number you can
create with the digits?　　　　　　　　　　_____　　[2]

3 Circle two numbers which add up to 100.

　　15　　　25　　　35　　　55　　　75　　　95　　　　　　[1]

4 Circle two numbers which have a difference of 2.5

　　0.5　　　1.0　　　1.5　　　2.0　　　2.5　　　3.0　　　[1]

5 Here is part of a number line.

　　　　　　　　1401　　1402　　1403　　1404　　1405

What value does the arrow point to?　　　　_____　　[1]

6 Hannah has £3 in 20 pence coins in her purse.
Circle the number of coins in Hannah's purse.

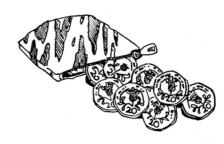

　　3　　　6　　　15　　　20　　　30　　　　　　　　　　[1]

Measuring Success in Maths: Year 4 © Jenny Lawson 2008. GL Assessment Limited

7 Complete these multiplications.

a   1   9
   ×   5
———
   5   ....
....
———
....   5
———

b   2   2
   ×   7
———
....   0
....
———
....   4
———

 3

8 Put the numbers 12, 15 and 22 in their correct places in this Venn diagram.

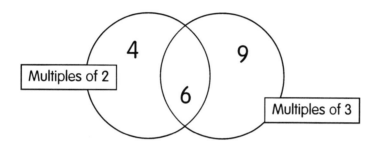

Multiples of 2   4   9   Multiples of 3
6

1

9 Mai was saving up for her holiday. In January, she saved £1. Then, each month, she doubled how much she saved.

a How much did she save in May?   £_____

b How much had she saved altogether
by the end of June?   £_____   **2**

10 Khalid's mum helped at a car boot sale.
She puts these items on a table.

Rewrite the prices in order.
Start with the highest.

    Highest

1

Name _____ Class _____ Date _____

1 Complete these sums.

a 100 x [ ] = 3700   **b** 430 ÷ [ ] = 43   [ ] **2**

2 Insert the symbols < or > to make these statements correct.

a 2 [ ] 6   **b** −3 [ ] −5   [ ] **2**

3 Fill in the missing numbers in this sequence.

| 4 | 8 | | | 20 | |

[ ] **1**

4 Fill in the missing numbers in this sequence.

| 12 | | | 3 | 0 | |

[ ] **1**

5 Here is part of a number line.

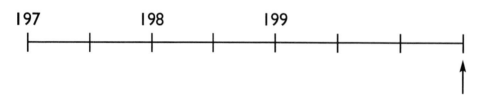

197   198   199

What value does the arrow point to?   _____ [ ] **1**

6 Put a number in each box to make this multiplication correct.

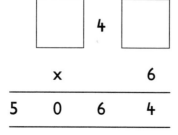

[ ] × [4] [ ]

```
        [ ]  4  [ ]
      ×          6
    _____
      5   0   6   4
    _____
```

[ ] **1**

Measuring Success in Maths: Year 4 © Jenny Lawson 2008. GL Assessment Limited

7 Jake and Mai are playing a number game.
They started with different numbers. They both got the same answer.
Jake started with 18.

Jake   Mai

What was Mai's starting number?   _____ | | 1 |

8 Mai made some mistakes in these sums.

a

```
      2   7   3
  +   1   4   8
  _____
      3   2   1
  _____
```

b

```
      4   6   2
  -   3   4   9
  _____
      8   1   1
  _____
```

What should her answers have been?   **a** _____

                                          b _____ | | 2 |

9 Here is a diagram for sorting numbers.

	Even	Not even
less than 20	14, 16	15, 17
not less than 20	24, 26	25, 29

Put the numbers 9, 10, 27 and 28 in their correct places in the table. | | 1 |

10 Khalid uses his calculator to work out three sums.

a He presses these keys:

What will the display show?

b He presses these keys:

What will the display show?

c He presses these keys:

What will the display show? | | 3 |

Block B — Securing number facts, understanding shape

Mental Maths Test

There are 15 questions in this test. Listen carefully to each question and then write down your answer.

5 seconds

		Answers
(1)	Write the number twelve hundred and two in figures.	1202
(2)	What is sixty-three divided by seven?	9
(3)	What is half of forty-six?	23
(4)	How many sides does a rectangle have?	4
(5)	Imagine a cube. How many faces does it have?	6

10 seconds

(6)	What is double twenty-nine?	58
(7)	In an equilateral triangle, two of the sides are five centimetres long. How long is the third side?	5 cm
(8)	What is half of eight hundred and twenty?	410
(9)	What is ten times forty-six?	460
(10)	Round the number three hundred and twenty-eight to the nearest ten.	330

15 seconds

(11)	A square-based pyramid has five faces. One face is a square. What shape are the other four faces?	triangular
(12)	A recipe says: use half fat to flour. Hannah uses forty grams of flour. How much fat should she use?	20 g
(13)	How many five hundred millilitre glasses could be filled from a litre of juice?	2
(14)	Mai walks six miles every day. How far does she walk in one week?	42 miles
(15)	Which three coins make seventeen pence?	10p, 5p and 2p

Measuring Success in Maths: Year 4 © Jenny Lawson 2008. GL Assessment Limited

There are 15 questions in this test. Listen carefully to each question and then write down your answer.

5 seconds	**Answers**
① Write the number fourteen hundred and two in figures.	1402
② What is nine hundred and fifty divided by ten?	95
③ What is half of thirty-six?	18
④ What is double forty-seven?	94
⑤ What is half of three hundred and twenty?	160

10 seconds	
⑥ Subtract twelve from fifty-eight.	46
⑦ A shape has six sides. What is it called?	hexagon
⑧ Imagine a square-based pyramid. How many faces does it have?	5
⑨ A triangular prism has five faces. Two faces are triangles. What shape are the other three faces?	rectangular
⑩ Round the number two hundred and thirty-two to the nearest ten.	230

15 seconds	
⑪ Ten grams of coffee powder make five cups of coffee. How many cups can be made from forty grams of coffee powder?	20
⑫ A rectangle has two sides four centimetres long and one side six centimetres long. How long is the fourth side?	6 cm
⑬ Mai runs seven miles every day. How far does she run in a week?	49 miles
⑭ Khalid can jog one mile in eight minutes. How far can he jog in twenty-four minutes?	3 miles
⑮ Which three coins make sixteen pence?	10p, 5p and 1p

Mental Maths Test

There are 15 questions in this test. Listen carefully to each question and then write down your answer.

5 seconds

		Answers
(1)	Write the number fifteen hundred and six in figures.	1506
(2)	What is eighty times seven?	560
(3)	What is half of thirty-four?	17
(4)	What is double thirty-eight?	76
(5)	What is half of two hundred and twenty?	110

10 seconds

(6)	Add thirty-three and sixteen.	49
(7)	A shape has five sides. What is it called?	pentagon
(8)	Imagine a triangular prism. How many faces does it have?	5
(9)	A cube has six square faces. How many edges does it have?	12
(10)	Round the number four hundred and fifty-five to the nearest ten.	460

15 seconds

(11)	Jake has sixty kilograms of fertiliser. He uses a kilogram a month for a year. How much fertiliser does he have left?	48 kg
(12)	In an isosceles triangle, the longest side is six centimetres long. One of the shorter sides is four centimetres long. How long is the other side?	4 cm
(13)	Khalid cycles four miles every day. How far does he cycle in one week?	28 miles
(14)	Hannah can swim one length of the pool in fifteen seconds. How many lengths can she swim in one minute?	4
(15)	Which three coins make fourteen pence?	10p, 2p and 2p

Measuring Success in Maths: Year 4 © Jenny Lawson 2008. GL Assessment Limited

Mental Maths Test B___

Name _____

Write the answer to each question in the space provided.

5 seconds

1		
2		
3		
4		
5		

10 seconds

6		
7		
8		
9		
10		

15 seconds

11		
12		
13		
14		
15		

Mental Maths Test B___

Name _____

Write the answer to each question in the space provided.

5 seconds

1		
2		
3		
4		
5		

10 seconds

6		
7		
8		
9		
10		

15 seconds

11		
12		
13		
14		
15		

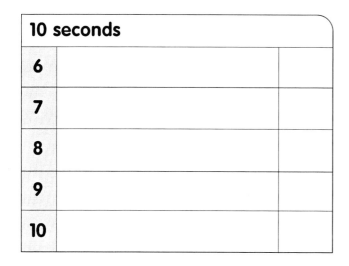

Name _____ Class _____ Date _____

1 Draw a line to link each triangle to the correct name.

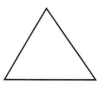 

right-angled triangle   isosceles triangle   equilateral triangle   ▢ **1**

2 Draw a trapezium on this grid.

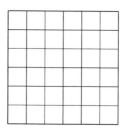

▢ **1**

3 A square has 4 equal sides.

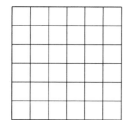

a Draw a square with side length 3 on this grid.

b Write one other fact that is true for all squares.

▢ **2**

4 Jake, Mai, Khalid and Hannah each draw a 2-D shape. Circle the rhombus.

A   B    C   D   ▢ **1**

5 Look at these 2-D shapes. Circle the pentagon.

A   B   C    D 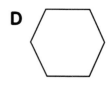   ▢ **1**

6 Draw a regular hexagon on this grid.

▢ **1**

Measuring Success in Maths: Year 4 © Jenny Lawson 2008. GL Assessment Limited

7 Jake, Mai, Khalid and Hannah each draw a 3-D shape.
Draw a line to link each shape to the person who drew it.

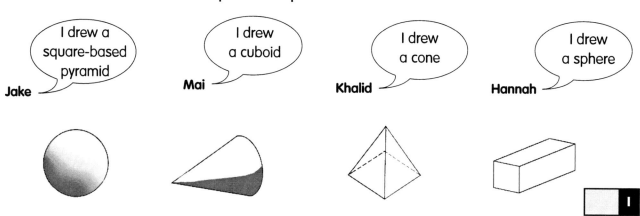

Jake: I drew a square-based pyramid
Mai: I drew a cuboid
Khalid: I drew a cone
Hannah: I drew a sphere

| | 1 |

8 Circle the shape that has a correct line of symmetry.

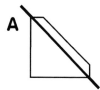 A   B   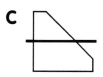 C   D

| | 1 |

9 Draw the lines of symmetry on each of these shapes.

| | 2 |

10 Complete this crossword using these words. 4 Across and 7 Down have already been completed.

circle   cube   octagon   parallelogram
rhombus   square   trapezium   pentagon

Across
3 A shape with all four sides the same length
4 A shape with four right angles
6 A shape with no straight sides
8 A shape with two sets of parallel lines
9 Also called a diamond
10 A shape with 5 sides

Down
1 Quadrilateral with only one pair of parallel sides
2 Solid with six square faces
5 A shape with eight sides
7 A shape with three sides

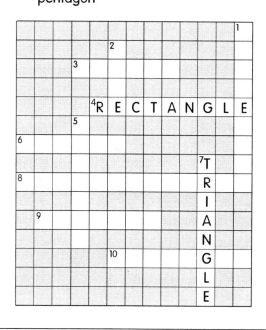

| | 4 |

Name _____ **Class** _____ **Date** _____

1 Mai has drawn a triangle inside a circle. Circle the name of the triangle.

equilateral   isosceles   scalene

| 1 |

2 Khalid has drawn a quadrilateral inside a right angled triangle.

a Circle the name of the quadrilateral.

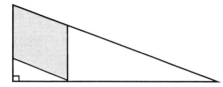

rectangle   square

trapezium   rhombus

b Write one fact about the quadrilateral.

| 2 |

3 What is the special name for the shape that this net makes?

_____

| 1 |

4 Which of these is not a net for a cube?

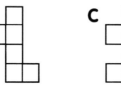

A   B   C   D

_____

| 1 |

5 Circle the two shapes that would fit together to make a rectangle.

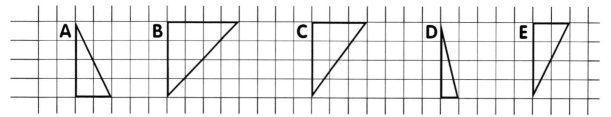

| 1 |

6 Circle the two shapes that would fit together to make a square.

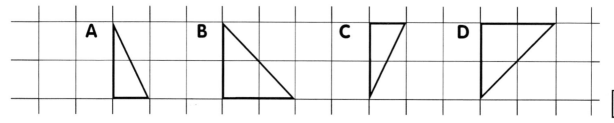

| 1 |

30

7 Jake, Mai, Khalid and Hannah each draw a 2-D shape.
Draw a line to link each shape to the person who drew it.

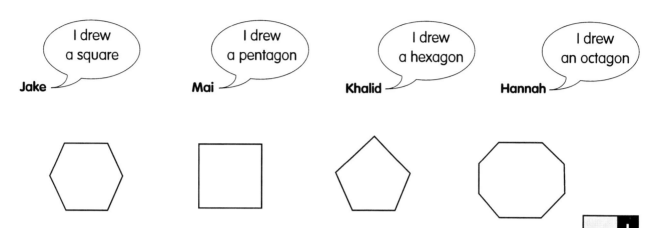

I drew a square   Jake

I drew a pentagon   Mai

I drew a hexagon   Khalid

I drew an octagon   Hannah

```
1
```

8 Mai has bought two presents. Write the name of the 3-D shape that describes each present.

a

b

_____   _____

```
2
```

9 Circle the two shapes that would fit together to make a square.

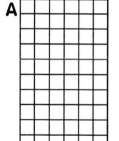 A   B 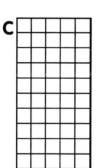 C   D   E 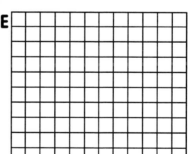   F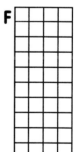

```
1
```

10 Draw the lines of symmetry on each of these shapes.

    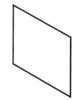   

```
4
```

Name _____ Class _____ Date _____

1 Hannah is trying to make sense of this number sentence:

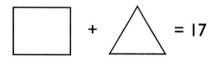

$$\square + \triangle = 17$$

She thinks of one possibility and checks her answer by filling in the table.

a Complete the next row of the table by suggesting another possibility.

b Complete the final row of the table with another suggestion.

□	△	Check
10	7	10 + 7 = 17

2

2 Mai has drawn a triangle inside a circle.
Circle the name of the triangle.

equilateral   isosceles   scalene

1

3 Khalid has drawn a quadrilateral inside a circle.
Circle the name of the quadrilateral.

rectangle   kite   trapezium   rhombus

1

4 Hannah drew this net. What shape will the net make?

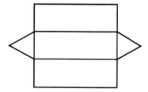

_____

1

5 Which of these nets does not make a square-based pyramid?

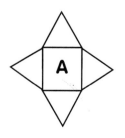

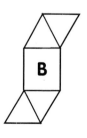

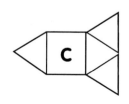

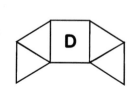

1

Measuring Success in Maths: Year 4 © Jenny Lawson 2008. GL Assessment Limited

6 This cube has a pattern on three of its faces.
Jake, Mai, Khalid and Hannah drew nets for this cube.
Circle all the correct nets for a cube.

A 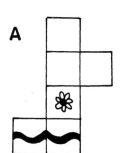   B 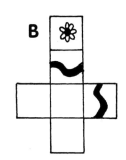   C 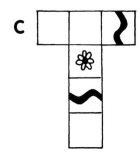   D 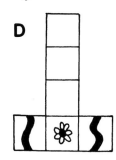   `2`

7 Circle the letter shapes that have reflective symmetry.

B C K L   `2`

8 Which two shapes fit together to make a parallelogram?_____

   `1`

9 Which two shapes fit together to make a trapezium? _____

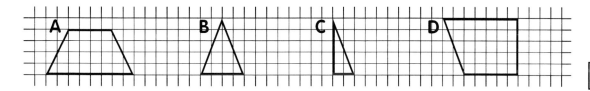   `1`

10 There are 6 chocolates left in this box. The 3 shaded shapes are chocolates wrapped in foil.

- The foil wrapped toffee is between the truffle and the marshmallow.
- The fudge is not foil wrapped.
- The nut cluster is foil wrapped but is not square.
- The coffee cream is not next to the marshmallow.

Put a **T** where the toffee is.
Put an **N** where the nut cluster is.
Put an **M** where the marshmallow is.

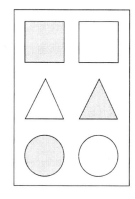   `3`

Block C — Handling data and measures

Mental Maths Test C1

There are 15 questions in this test. Listen carefully to each question and then write down your answer.

5 seconds	**Answers**
① Write the number two thousand and six in figures.	2006
② Multiply nine by seven.	63
③ What is eight squared?	64
④ Write nought point one as a fraction.	$\frac{1}{10}$
⑤ How many grams are there in one kilogram?	1000

10 seconds |
--- | ---
⑥ How many millilitres are there in one litre? | 1000
⑦ How many metres are there in three kilometres? | 3000
⑧ How many centimetres are there in one point two metres? | 120
⑨ Write seventeen millimetres to the nearest centimetre. | 2 cm
⑩ What is four plus seven plus nine? | 20

15 seconds |
--- | ---
⑪ Which is more: two hundred and fifty millilitres or nought point five litres? | 0.5 litres
⑫ What length is half way between four centimetres and five centimetres? | 4.5 cm
⑬ How many two hundred and fifty millilitre glasses can be filled from a jug holding one litre of juice? | 4
⑭ Ribbon costs two pounds per metre. How much will fifty centimetres cost? | £1
⑮ Hannah has four metres of rope. She cuts off fifty centimetres. How much rope does she have left, in metres? | 3.5 m

Measuring Success in Maths: Year 4 © Jenny Lawson 2008. GL Assessment Limited

There are 15 questions in this test. Listen carefully to each question and then write down your answer.

5 seconds	**Answers**
① Write the number three thousand and sixty in figures.	3060
② Multiply nine by six.	54
③ What is seven squared?	49
④ Write nought point five as a fraction.	$\frac{1}{2}$
⑤ How many centimetres are there in one metre?	100

10 seconds	
⑥ How many grams are there in half a kilogram?	500
⑦ How many metres are there in two kilometres?	2000
⑧ How many millimetres are there in twenty-five centimetres?	250
⑨ Write twenty-nine millimetres to the nearest centimetre.	3 cm
⑩ Which is heavier: two thousand grams or three kilograms?	3 kg

15 seconds	
⑪ What is thirteen plus twelve plus nine?	34
⑫ What distance is half way between four kilometres and five kilometres?	4.5 km
⑬ How many twenty-five centimetre ribbons can be cut from a strip one metre long?	4
⑭ Sugar costs one pound per kilogram. How much will two hundred and fifty grams cost?	25p
⑮ Khalid has one litre of juice. He drinks five hundred millilitres. How much juice is left, in litres?	0.5 litres or $\frac{1}{2}$ litre

There are 15 questions in this test. Listen carefully to each question and then write down your answer.

5 seconds	**Answers**
(1) Write the number four thousand and fourteen in figures.	4014
(2) Multiply nine by eight.	72
(3) What is six squared?	36
(4) Write nought point nought one as a fraction.	$\frac{1}{100}$
(5) How many millimetres are there in a centimetre?	10

10 seconds	
(6) How many milligrams are there in a gram?	1000
(7) How many millilitres are there in two litres?	2000
(8) How many grams are there in two kilograms?	2000
(9) Write one thousand seven hundred grams to the nearest kilogram.	2 kg
(10) What height is half way between two metres and three metres?	2.5 m

15 seconds	
(11) What is twelve plus fourteen plus nine?	35
(12) Rope costs two pounds per metre. How much will two hundred and fifty centimetres cost?	50p
(13) Mai has one kilogram of sugar. She uses five hundred grams in a recipe. How much sugar, in kilograms, does she have left?	0.5 kg or $\frac{1}{2}$ kg
(14) Which is longer: a quarter of a kilometre or five hundred metres?	500 m
(15) If I have one kilogram of dough, how many twenty-five gram bread rolls can I make?	40

   Measuring Success in Maths: Year 4 © Jenny Lawson 2008. GL Assessment Limited

Mental Maths Test C

Mental Maths Test C

Name	

Name	

Write the answer to each question in the space provided.

Write the answer to each question in the space provided.

5 seconds

1		
2		
3		
4		
5		

10 seconds

6		
7		
8		
9		
10		

15 seconds

11		
12		
13		
14		
15		

5 seconds

1		
2		
3		
4		
5		

10 seconds

6		
7		
8		
9		
10		

15 seconds

11		
12		
13		
14		
15		

Name _____ Class _____ Date _____

1 How many millilitres make 1 litre?

_____ ml   [ ] **1**

2 Complete these statements.

 a 2 km = [   ] m   **b** 175 cm = [   ] m   [ ] **2**

3 Complete these statements.

 a 1 kg = [   ] g   **b** 700 g = [   ] kg   [ ] **2**

4 Mai is making a cake.
How much flour has she put
on the scales?

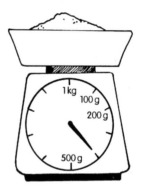

_____   [ ] **1**

5 Here is part of a tape measure.

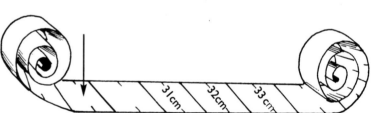

What length does the arrow point to?   _____   [ ] **1**

6 This table shows children's activities at an adventure park.

How many more children went cycling than ice skating in July?

	June	July	August
swimming	20	55	80
cycling	40	30	25
ice skating	10	20	20

_____   [ ] **1**

Measuring Success in Maths: Year 4 © Jenny Lawson 2008. GL Assessment Limited

7) Hannah collected information about the colours of some pens being used in class. Here are her results.

Fill in the missing labels on both axes of the bar chart.

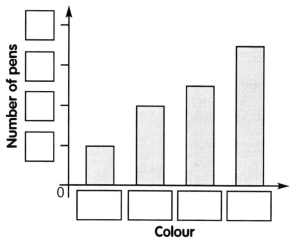

Colour	Number of pens
red (r)	2
yellow (y)	7
blue (b)	5
green (g)	4

2

8) This chart shows the sports teams that Jake, Mai, Khalid and Hannah belong to.

a Who belongs to the most teams? _____

b Who does not belong to the cycling team? _____

	Jake	Mai	Khalid	Hannah
rounders	✓			
swimming		✓		
tennis	✓			
cycling	✓		✓	✓
football	✓	✓		✓

2

9) Jake and Mai travel to school by bus. This table shows the old and new bus fares on their routes.

a Jake's old fare was £1.20
How much did it increase? _____ p

b Mai's fare has increased the least.
How much was her old fare? _____

Old bus fare	New bus fare
40p	45p
64p	70p
76p	85p
92p	£1.05
£1.05	£1.20
£1.20	£1.40

2

10) The children in Hannah's class stand in a line, from shortest to tallest.

How can Hannah find out how many in her class are taller than her?

Jake — (Count the number of people in the class)

Mai — (Count the number of people on her left)

Khalid — (Count the number of people on her right)

Hannah

Who is correct? _____

1

Name _____ Class _____ Date _____

1 Complete these statements.

a 1 km = ☐ m   **b** ☐ m = $\frac{1}{2}$ km   `2`

2 Complete these statements.

a 2 litres = ☐ ml   **b** 175 ml = ☐ litres   `2`

3 Complete these statements.

a 1.5 kg = ☐ g   **b** 70 g = ☐ kg   `2`

4 Mai has a ribbon which is 4 m long. She cuts it in half.

How long is each piece of ribbon?   _____   `1`

5 Khalid packs a case of clothes for his holiday. It weighs 21 kg. The airline baggage limit is 20 kg.

How many grams of clothing will Khalid need to remove from his suitcase?

_____   `1`

6 Hannah belongs to a drama group. This bar chart shows how many people came to see their latest play.

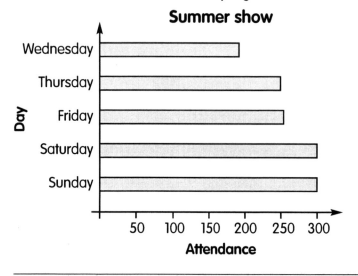

Each person paid £1 for a ticket. How much was collected on the Friday?

_____   `1`

Measuring Success in Maths: Year 4 © Jenny Lawson 2008. GL Assessment Limited

(7) Add these numbers to the Venn diagram: 97, 98, 120.

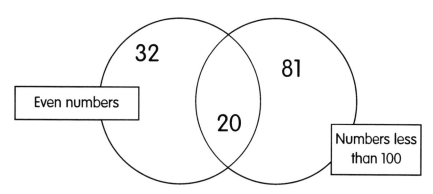

8   This table shows children's activities at an adventure park.

	June	July	August
swimming	20	55	80
cycling	40	30	25
ice skating	10	20	20

How many children went cycling in July and August in total?

_____ | **I**

9   This pie chart shows how Year 4 children at Jake's school travel to school.

30 children in Year 4 walk to school.

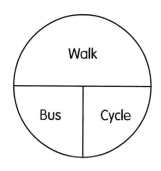

a   How many children are there in Year 4?   _____

b   How many children travel by bus?   _____

c   How many children cycle?   _____ | **3**

10   Mai thinks that most children in her class walk to school.
Write down one question she could ask to find out if she is right.

  | **I**

C3

Name _____ Class _____ Date _____

① Complete the statement.

$\frac{1}{4}$ litre = [   ] ml

 1

② Complete these statements.

a 3.5 km = [   ] m   **b** 2500 cm = [   ] m

 2

③ Complete these statements.

a 0.25 kg = [   ] g   **b** 50 g = [   ] kg

 2

④ Jake walks the 500 m from his home to his school.
Mai lives twice as far away from school as Jake.
Khalid lives twice as far away from school as Mai.

How far is Khalid's house from school, in km?   _____

 1

⑤ Khalid is making fruit punch. He puts
fruit juice, ice and lemon into this jug.

He fills the jug with lemonade.

How much lemonade will be
left in the lemonade bottle? _____

1

⑥ Mai is making pastry for a pie and uses half as much fat as flour.

She uses 450 g of flour. How much fat should she use?   _____

 1

⑦ This pie chart shows the favourite pop groups of
Year 4 children at Jake's school.

25 children in Year 4 chose the Bright Beams.

a How many chose the Arty Ants?_____

b How many do not choose
the Clever Clogs?   _____

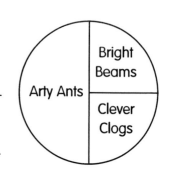

2

Measuring Success in Maths: Year 4 © Jenny Lawson 2008. GL Assessment Limited

8 Jake and Mai looked for insects in their gardens for one week. They each made a pie chart of what they saw.

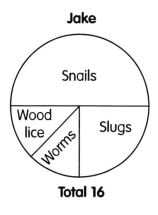

Jake

Total 16

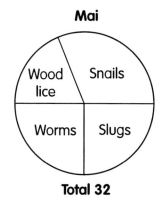

Mai

Total 32

a Who saw the most snails?

_____

b Estimate how many worms Jake saw.

_____

[2]

9 This chart shows the amount of money spent in a clothes shop in four sales.

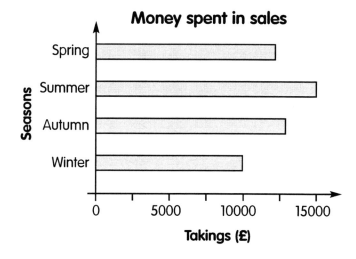

a How much was spent in the Spring sale? _____

b How much more was spent in the Summer sale than in the Winter sale? _____

[2]

10 Jake wants to find out the distances that his classmates travel to school and the type of transport they use. Mai, Khalid and Hannah suggest questions he should ask to find out.

Ask everyone in the class how far they live from the school

Mai

Ask everyone in the class how they come to school: by car or by bus or walking

Khalid

Ask everyone in the class how they come to school and how far away they live

Hannah

Who is right? _____

[1]

Mental Maths Test   D1

There are 15 questions in this test. Listen carefully to each question and then write down your answer.

5 seconds	**Answers**
① Write the number nineteen thousand and fifty-one in figures.	19,051
② How many twenty pence coins have the same value as one pound?	5
③ One side of a square is two metres long. How long is the perimeter?	8 m
④ One side of a regular hexagon is three metres long. How long is the perimeter?	18 m
⑤ The time is a quarter to seven in the evening. Write this as it would appear on a twenty-four hour digital clock.	18:45

10 seconds	
⑥ A square has an area of forty-nine square centimetres. What is the length of one side?	7 cm
⑦ A fence surrounds a rectangular garden which is ten metres by five metres in size. How long is the fence?	30 m
⑧ You have seventy pence. Oranges cost nine pence each. How many oranges could you buy?	7
⑨ Mai is saving up for a holiday. She puts one pound twenty away each week for five weeks. How much has she saved?	£6
⑩ A TV programme starts at a quarter past seven. It lasts for twenty minutes. At what time does it end?	7:35

15 seconds	
⑪ Mai is one hundred and thirty centimetres tall. Her sister is forty-seven centimetres shorter. How tall is Mai's sister?	83 cm
⑫ In a long journey, Jake drove fifty-eight kilometres before lunch and two hundred and thirty-eight kilometres after lunch. How far did he drive altogether?	296 km
⑬ I have forty pence. My friend has twice as much as me. How much do we have altogether?	£1.20
⑭ Khalid is facing north. He turns clockwise through three right angles. Which direction is he facing now?	west
⑮ You buy three cans of drink, costing ninety-five pence each. How much change should you receive from a five pound note?	£2.15

Measuring Success in Maths: Year 4 © Jenny Lawson 2008. GL Assessment Limited

There are 15 questions in this test. Listen carefully to each question and then write down your answer.

5 seconds	**Answers**
1. Write the number eighteen thousand and fifty in figures.	18,050
2. Five people share a bill of fifteen pounds equally. How much do they each pay?	£3
3. The time is a half-past six in the evening. Write this as it would appear on a twenty-four hour digital clock.	18:30
4. If one mouse mat costs one pound ninety-five, how much would two mouse mats cost?	£3.90
5. A jar of jam normally costs ninety pence. What is the saving if you buy two jars on a buy-one-get-one-free offer?	90p

10 seconds	
6. How many fifty pence pieces have the same value as a five pound note?	10
7. The time is one a.m. What time was it three hours ago?	10 p.m.
8. A meal costs four pounds sixty-five. What change should you get from five pounds?	35p
9. You have sixty pence. Apples cost sixteen pence each. How many apples could you buy?	3
10. Each side of a regular shape is three centimetres long. The perimeter is fifteen centimetres. What is the shape?	pentagon

15 seconds	
11. A t-shirt costs two pounds seventy-five. You buy three. How much change should you have from ten pounds?	£1.75
12. Two shelves are seventy-five and eighty-seven centimetres long. What is their total length?	1.62 m or 162 cm
13. Khalid earns sixteen pounds a week doing a paper round. He saves half his earnings. How much has he saved after eight weeks?	£64
14. One length of the swimming pool is twenty-five metres. Hannah swims two hundred and twenty-five metres in the pool. How many lengths does she swim?	9
15. A breakfast television programme starts at ten past nine. It lasts for forty minutes. At what time does it end?	9:50

There are 15 questions in this test. Listen carefully to each question and then write down your answer.

5 seconds | Answers

1. Write the number seventeen thousand and forty-nine in figures. | 17,049
2. How many ten pence coins have the same value as four twenty pence pieces? | 8
3. Jake saves two pounds fifty for four weeks. How much does he save? | £10
4. The time is ten to seven in the evening.
   Write this as it would appear on a twenty-four hour digital clock. | 18:50
5. The time is three p.m. What time was it four hours ago? | 11 a.m.

10 seconds

6. Jelly beans cost seventy pence for one hundred grams.
   What is the cost of one hundred and fifty grams of jelly beans? | £1.05
7. A taxi ride costs two pounds eighty. You give the driver three pounds saying 'keep the change'. How much did you tip? | 20p
8. You buy two bars of chocolate costing forty-five pence each.
   How much change should you receive from one pound? | 10p
9. Each side of a regular shape is two centimetres long.
   The perimeter is twelve centimetres. What is the shape? | hexagon
10. Shampoo normally costs one pound ninety-five a bottle. How much could you save, by buying two bottles on a buy-one-get-one-free offer? | £1.95

15 seconds

11. Two shelves are thirty-five and seventy-eight centimetres long.
    What's the difference between their lengths? | 43 cm
12. Mai is facing north-west. She turns clockwise through two right angles.
    Which direction is she facing now? | south-east
13. I have thirty pence. My friend has three times as much as me.
    How much do we have altogether? | £1.20
14. A bar of chocolate costs one pound thirty-six.
    Jake and Mai share the cost equally. How much do they each pay? | 68p
15. A breakfast television programme starts at a quarter to eight.
    It lasts for twenty minutes. At what time does it end? | 8:05

Measuring Success in Maths: Year 4 © Jenny Lawson 2008. GL Assessment Limited

Mental Maths Test D___

Name _____

Write the answer to each question in the space provided.

5 seconds

1		
2		
3		
4		
5		

10 seconds

6		
7		
8		
9		
10		

15 seconds

11		
12		
13		
14		
15		

Mental Maths Test D___

Name _____

Write the answer to each question in the space provided.

5 seconds

1		
2		
3		
4		
5		

10 seconds

6		
7		
8		
9		
10		

15 seconds

11		
12		
13		
14		
15		

Measuring Success in Maths: Year 4 © Jenny Lawson 2008. GL Assessment Limited

Name _____ Class _____ Date _____

1 What time is shown on the clock face, to the nearest minute?

_____ ☐ I

2 Circle the smallest angle.

  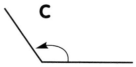 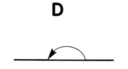

☐ I

3 What is the size of angle *x* in this diagram?

_____ ☐ I

4 Which of these shapes is **not** a rectangle?

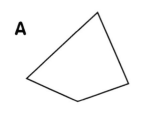 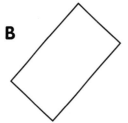 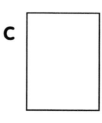 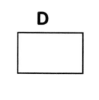

_____ ☐ 1

5 What is the area of this shape?

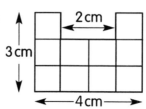

_____ ☐ I

6 Mai starts at E5 on the grid.
She moves 3 squares north and
then 2 squares west.

Which square is she in now? _____

☐ I

Measuring Success in Maths: Year 4 © Jenny Lawson 2008. GL Assessment Limited

7 Hannah is baking a cake. She puts flour on the scales and then adds sugar.

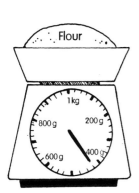

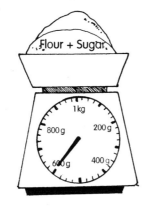

How much sugar does she add?

_____ | 1 |

8 Hannah empties her purse.

a How many coins were in the purse?

_____

b How much money was in the purse ?

_____ | 2 |

9 This table shows the details of the bus route from Eastlea to Westlea.

Bus depot: Eastlea	12:00
Garden Hill	12:25
The Park	12:35
Lakeview	12:50
Bus depot: Westlea	13:00

a How long does the bus take to travel from Eastlea to The Park?

_____

b How long does it take from Lakeview to Westlea?   _____

c How long does it take from Eastlea to Westlea?   _____ | 3 |

10 Look at this map.

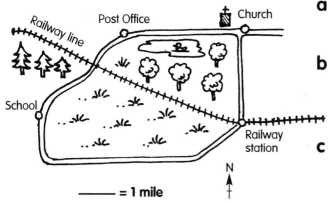

____ = 1 mile

a What is to the north-east of the School?   _____

b How far is it from the Railway station to the Church?

_____ miles

c What direction is the Railway station from the Church?

_____ | 3 |

D2

① Shade three more boxes to create a horizontal rectangular shape on this grid.

4			
3			
2			
1			
	A	B	C	D

② Khalid starts on square D4, facing West. He walks forward 2 squares, turns through 180 degrees and then walks forward 5 squares.

Which square is he in now? _____

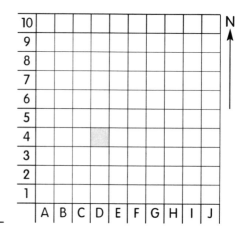

③ Look at this shape. Circle the shape that has the same area.

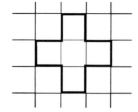

A   B   C   D

④ Which statement describes this rectangle?

A Its perimeter is 7 cm and its area is 12 cm².
B Its perimeter is 14 cm and its area is 12 cm².
C Its perimeter is 12 cm and its area is 14 cm².
D Its perimeter is 14 cm and its area is 6 cm².

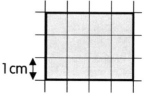

1 cm

⑤ What size is angle *x* in this semicircle?

Circle the correct angle.

   90°   180°   210°   270°

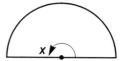

x

⑥ Which diagram shows the correct reflection of the flag in the mirror?

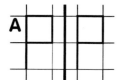 A

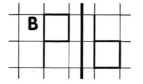 B

 C

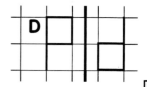 D

Measuring Success in Maths: Year 4 © Jenny Lawson 2008. GL Assessment Limited

(7) Mai used four small squares and one large square to make this shape.

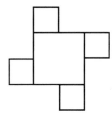

　　a How many small squares would fit into
　　　　the larger square? _____

　　b The sides of the small squares are 1 cm.
　　　　What is the perimeter of Mai's shape? _____ 　| 2 |

(8) Khalid has £2 to make a telephone call.

He spends these coins making the call.

　　a How much does the call cost? _____

　　b How much change does Khalid have after he
　　　　has made the call? _____ 　| 2 |

(9) These are the opening times of the swimming pool.

　　a How long is the pool open for
　　　　on Wednesdays?

　　　　_____

OPENING TIMES			
	Morning		**Afternoon**
Monday	09:00	to	19:30
Tuesday/Thursday/Friday	10:30	to	19:30
Wednesday	10:30	to	13:00
Saturday	09:00	to	12:30
Sunday	Pool closed		

　　b Khalid arrives at the pool at
　　　　11:50 on Saturday.
　　　　How many **minutes** is it
　　　　before the pool closes?

　　　　_____ 　| 2 |

(10) Look at this map.

　　a What is south-west of the Post Office?

　　　　_____

　　b How far is it from the Post Office
　　　　to the Church?

　　　　_____ miles

　　c What direction is the Church
　　　　from the Railway station?

　　　　_____

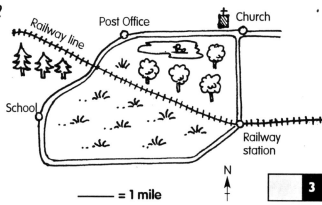

N

——— = 1 mile

| 3 |

D3 ✓✓✓

Name _____ Class _____ Date _____

(1) Look at these lengths.

0.1 km   0.56 m   3.6 m   125 m   125 cm

a Which is the shortest length?   _____

b Which is the longest length?   _____ | **2** |

(2) Shade three more boxes on this grid to fill a column.

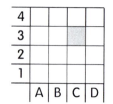

| **1** |

(3)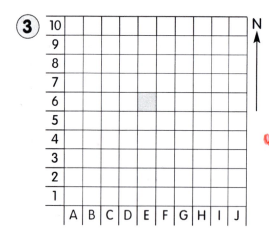

Jake starts at E6 on the grid. He moves 2 squares north.
He turns right and moves forward 5 squares.

Where is he now?   _____ | **1** |

(4) Circle the shape that has the same area as this shape.

 A **B** 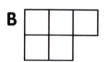 **C**  **D**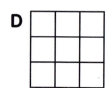

| **1** |

(5) What is the area of this shape?

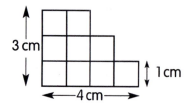

3 cm

1 cm

←— 4 cm —→

_____ cm² | **1** |

Measuring Success in Maths: Year 4 © Jenny Lawson 2008. GL Assessment Limited

6 These shapes are drawn on a centimetre grid.
Circle the shape with an area of 15 cm².

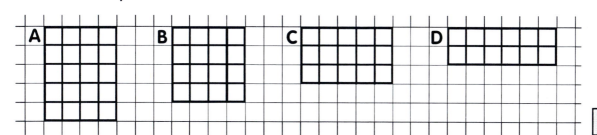

⬜ **1**

7 Look at this design and complete the sentence using one of these words:

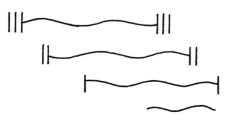

horizontal   vertical

All the wavy lines are _____

⬜ **1**

8 Jake makes a rectangular design using 5 tiles.

Each tile ⬜ is 2 cm by 4 cm.

a What is the width of his design?   _____

b What is the height of his design?   _____

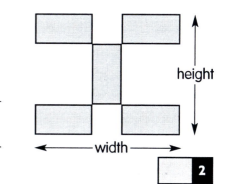

⬜ **2**

9 Khalid has made this L shape using some square tiles.

a What is the perimeter of the L shape? _____

b What is the area of the L shape?   _____

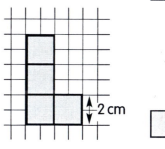

⬜ **2**

10 Look at this map.

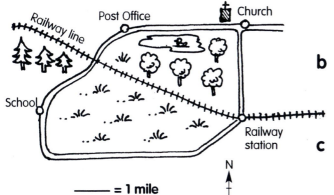

—— = 1 mile

N

a What is west of the Railway station?

_____

b How far is it from the School to Railway station?

_____ miles

c What direction is the Post Office from the School?

_____

⬜ **3**

Block E

Securing number facts, relationships and calculating

Mental Maths Test

There are 15 questions in this test. Listen carefully to each question and then write down your answer.

5 seconds	**Answers**
① Write the number forty thousand and sixty-eight in figures.	40,068
② Write the fraction one half as a decimal.	0.5
③ Write the decimal nought point seven five as a fraction.	$\frac{3}{4}$
④ How many pence are in nought point two five pounds?	25
⑤ What is two times one-third?	$\frac{2}{3}$

10 seconds	
⑥ Two fractions add up to one. One of them is a fifth. What is the other one?	$\frac{4}{5}$
⑦ What is one-fifth of thirty-five metres?	7 m
⑧ What is one-third of sixty litres?	20 litres
⑨ There are exactly seven weeks until my birthday. How many days is that?	49 days
⑩ Which is the odd one out: one-half, two-quarters, three-sixths, four-ninths?	$\frac{4}{9}$

15 seconds	
⑪ One length of the swimming pool is twenty-five metres. Mai swims seven lengths of the pool. How far does she swim altogether?	175 m
⑫ My pencil-case has two red pencils for every three blue pencils. There are four red pencils. How many blue pencils are there?	6
⑬ There are ninety children at the cinema. There are half as many boys as girls. How many girls are there?	60
⑭ Mai puts five seeds in each of her pots. She uses six pots and has two seeds left over. How many seeds did she start off with?	32
⑮ Twenty-one marbles are shared between some children. Each child receives five marbles and there is one marble left over. How many children share the marbles?	4

Measuring Success in Maths: Year 4 © Jenny Lawson 2008. GL Assessment Limited

There are 15 questions in this test. Listen carefully to each question and then write down your answer.

5 seconds	**Answers**
(1) Write the number fifty thousand and thirty-two in figures.	50,032
(2) Write the fraction one-tenth as a decimal.	0.1
(3) Write the decimal nought point five as a fraction.	$\frac{1}{2}$
(4) What is two times one-fifth?	$\frac{2}{5}$
(5) What is one-sixth of thirty-six metres?	6 m

10 seconds	
(6) Two fractions add up to one. One of them is a third. What is the other one?	$\frac{2}{3}$
(7) What fraction of one metre is twenty-five centimetres?	$\frac{1}{4}$
(8) What is one-quarter of eighty litres?	20 litres
(9) There are fifty-six days until my holiday. How many weeks do I have to wait?	7 weeks
(10) Which is the odd one out: one-third, two-sixths, three-tenths, four-twelfths?	$\frac{3}{10}$

15 seconds	
(11) One length of the swimming pool is twenty-five metres. Mai swims nine lengths. How far does she swim altogether?	225 m
(12) My birthday cake has two red candles for every five blue candles. There are four red candles. How many blue candles are there?	10
(13) There are one hundred and fifty children at the cinema. There are half as many boys as girls. How many girls are there?	100
(14) Mai puts four seeds in each of her pots. She uses seven pots and has two seeds left over. How many seeds did she start off with?	30
(15) Twenty-seven marbles are shared between some children. Each child receives five marbles and there are two marbles left over. How many children share the marbles?	5

There are 15 questions in this test. Listen carefully to each question and then write down your answer.

5 seconds	**Answers**
(1) Write the number sixty thousand and sixty-six in figures.	60,066
(2) Write the fraction one hundredth as a decimal.	0.01
(3) Write the decimal nought point two five as a fraction.	$\frac{1}{4}$
(4) What is two times two-fifths?	$\frac{4}{5}$
(5) What fraction of one pound is twenty pence?	$\frac{1}{5}$

10 seconds	
(6) Two fractions add up to one. One is two-fifths. What's the other?	$\frac{3}{5}$
(7) What is one-third of thirty-three metres?	11 m
(8) What is one-fifth of fifty litres?	10 litres
(9) My birthday is on April the twenty-third. Today is April the second. How many weeks do I have to wait till my birthday?	3 weeks
(10) Which of these fractions is the odd one out: one-quarter, two-ninths, three-twelfths, four-sixteenths?	$\frac{2}{9}$

15 seconds	
(11) One length of the swimming pool is twenty-five metres. Mai swims ten lengths. How far does she swim altogether, in kilometres?	0.25 km
(12) My necklace has three red beads for every four blue beads. If there are nine red beads, how many blue beads are there?	12
(13) There are one hundred and twenty children at the cinema. There are half as many girls as boys. How many boys are there?	80
(14) Mai puts five seeds in each of her pots. She uses seven pots and has one seed left over. How many seeds did she start off with?	36
(15) Nineteen marbles are shared between some children. Each child receives three marbles and there is one marble left over. How many children share the marbles?	6

Measuring Success in Maths: Year 4 © Jenny Lawson 2008. GL Assessment Limited

Mental Maths Test

Mental Maths Test

Name _____

Name _____

Write the answer to each question in the space provided.

Write the answer to each question in the space provided.

5 seconds

1		
2		
3		
4		
5		

10 seconds

6		
7		
8		
9		
10		

15 seconds

11		
12		
13		
14		
15		

5 seconds

1		
2		
3		
4		
5		

10 seconds

6		
7		
8		
9		
10		

15 seconds

11		
12		
13		
14		
15		

Name _____ Class _____ Date _____

(1) Complete these sums.

a $\frac{1}{2}$ of 100 = ⬜   **b** $\frac{3}{4}$ of 100 = ⬜   ⬜ **2**

(2) True or false? Circle the correct answer.

a $\frac{9}{20}$ is greater than $\frac{1}{2}$ **true / false**

b $\frac{3}{11}$ is less than $\frac{1}{2}$ **true / false**   ⬜ **2**

(3) True or false? Circle the correct answer.

a 0.6 is greater than $\frac{1}{2}$ **true / false**

b 0.06 is less than $\frac{1}{2}$ **true / false**   ⬜ **2**

(4) Mai ate two slices of this cake.
Circle the fraction of the cake that she ate.

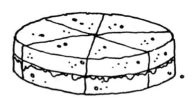

$$\frac{2}{1} \qquad \frac{1}{6} \qquad \frac{1}{3} \qquad \frac{3}{6} \qquad \frac{4}{6}$$

⬜ **1**

(5) Fill in the boxes to make each fraction equivalent to $\frac{1}{2}$.

$$\frac{1}{2} = \frac{6}{\Box} = \frac{\Box}{20} = \frac{9}{\Box}$$

⬜ **1**

(6) Complete these statements.

a For every 2 apples, there are
_____ bananas.

b For every 3 bananas, there are
_____ lemons.

⬜ **2**

58   *Measuring Success in Maths: Year 4* © Jenny Lawson 2008. GL Assessment Limited

7 Jake's sister, Lucy, is 7 years old. Their mother is 32 years old. Jake is trying to work out how many years older her mother is than Lucy.

Circle the calculation he could use to work out the answer.

| 39 − 32 | | 32 + 7 | | 32 x 7 | | 32 − 7 | | 39 − 7 |

8 If a number is divisible by three, the sum of its digits is also divisible by three.

$3 \times 7 = $ ㉑ $\longrightarrow$ $2 + 1 = 3$

$3 \times 13 = $ ㊴ $\longrightarrow$ $3 + 9 = $ ⑫ $\longrightarrow$ $1 + 2 = 3$

Circle all the numbers that are divisible by 3.

39   47   78   82   97

9 Which is more? Which is less?
Write > or < to make these statements true.

a 3 pizzas shared between 4 [ ] 6 pizzas shared between 10.

b 2 cakes shared between 5 [ ] 5 cakes shared between 10.

10 Circle the pair of shapes that shows one and one-third of this shape.

A

B

C

D

E2

Name _____ Class _____ Date _____

1 What number is Hannah thinking of?

One half of my
number is five

_____ ☐ 1

2 What number is Jake thinking of?

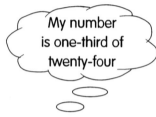

My number
is one-third of
twenty-four

_____ ☐ 1

3 Complete these sums.

a $\frac{1}{2}$ of 200 = ☐   **b** $\frac{3}{4}$ of 200 = ☐   2

4 Complete this sequence.

$\frac{1}{4}$ $\frac{1}{2}$ ☐   1 $1\frac{1}{4}$ ☐ $1\frac{3}{4}$ ☐   ☐ 1

5 Which is more? Which is less?
Write > or < in the boxes to make these statements true.

a $\frac{1}{5}$ of 30 sweets $\frac{3}{4}$ of 12 sweets

b $\frac{1}{4}$ of 40 sweets $\frac{1}{3}$ of 24 sweets   2

6 Fill in the boxes to make equivalent fractions.

$$\frac{1}{4} = \frac{6}{\boxed{}} = \frac{\boxed{}}{20} = \frac{9}{\boxed{}}$$

☐ 1

Measuring Success in Maths: Year 4 © Jenny Lawson 2008. GL Assessment Limited

7 Draw lines to connect fractions that add up to 1.

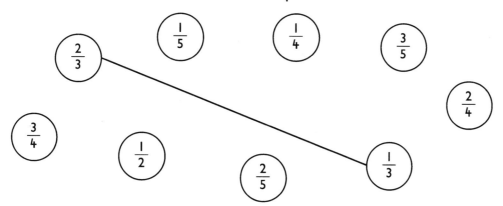

3

8 Mai has bricks of length 2. Hannah has bricks of length 3 and Jake has bricks of length 4.

They each place one brick on the same start line and then build a line of bricks using their own size bricks end to end.

They stop when all their lines are the same length.

How many bricks does Jake use? _____

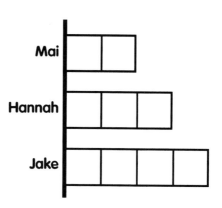

1

9 Circle the group of shapes that does not have three-quarters shaded.

A   B 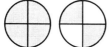   C    D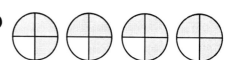

1

10 One quarter of the children in a class are girls. There are 8 girls.

a How many children are there in the class? _____

b How many boys are there in the class? _____

2

Name _____ Class _____ Date _____

1 What number is Khalid thinking of?

My number is ten times bigger than thirty-seven

_____ ☐ 1

2 Complete these sums.

a $\frac{1}{10}$ of 560 = ☐

b $\frac{1}{100}$ of 480 = ☐

☐ 2

3 Complete each multiplication fact and its division fact.

a 5 × 8 = ☐   40 ÷ 8 = ☐

b 7 × 9 = ☐   63 ÷ ☐ = 9

☐ 2

4 Fill in the boxes to make each of these fractions equivalent to $\frac{3}{4}$.

$$\frac{3}{4} = \frac{6}{\boxed{}} = \frac{\boxed{}}{20} = \frac{9}{\boxed{}}$$

☐ 1

5 Mai buys 3 small bags of sweets.
She gives the shop keeper £2 and is given 80p change.

a How much did Mai spend?   _____

b What is the cost of one bag of sweets?   _____ p   ☐ 2

6 In a book of stamps, there are 2 first-class stamps
to every 5 second-class stamps.
There are 15 second-class stamps in the book.

How many first-class stamps are there?   _____ ☐ 1

Measuring Success in Maths: Year 4 © Jenny Lawson 2008. GL Assessment Limited

7 Hannah is thinking of a number less than 30. She divides it by 4 and gets a remainder of 1.

If Hannah divides the **same** starting number by 5 she also gets a remainder of 1.

a   What number was Hannah thinking of?   _____

b   What number must she divide the same starting number by to get a remainder of 5?   _____ | 2 |

8 Two fractions that are the same as 0.25 are $\frac{1}{4}$ and $\frac{25}{100}$.
Are there any other possibilities?

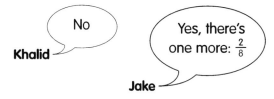

Khalid — No

Jake — Yes, there's one more: $\frac{2}{8}$

Mai — Yes, there are two more: $\frac{2}{8}$ and $\frac{3}{12}$

Hannah — Yes, there are loads more: any fraction with the top number a quarter of the bottom number

Who is right?   _____ | 1 |

9 This square is divided into three parts.

Part A is $\frac{1}{4}$ of the area of the square.

Part B is $\frac{1}{2}$ of the area of the square.

Which fraction of the area of the square is part C?

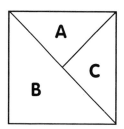

$\frac{1}{5}$ $\frac{1}{4}$ $\frac{1}{2}$ $\frac{2}{6}$ _____ | 1 |

10 One third of the children in a class are girls. There are 16 boys.

a   How many children are there in the class?

_____

b   How many girls are there in the class?

_____ | 2 |

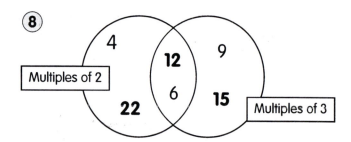

Answers   Written tests

Test A1   page 18

1. 9631
2. Jake
3. a 350   b 230
4. a 13   b 2
5. a any number < 7   b any number < 24
6. 3 x 6 and 9 x 2
7. a 350   b 449
8. a 92   b 78
9. 6
10.

	Even	Not even
less than 10	4, 6, **2**	5, 7, **1**
not less than 10	14, 18, **12**	15, 17, **19**

Test A2   page 20

1. a 630   b 71
2. a 1257   b 7521
3. 25 and 75
4. 0.5 and 3.0
5. 1399
6. 15
7. a
```
    1  9
  x    5
  -------
    5  0
    4  5
  -------
    9  5
```
   b
```
    2  2
  x    7
  -------
  1  4  0
     1  4
  -------
  1  5  4
```

[1 mark for each correct answer digit]

8.
```
Multiples of 2        Multiples of 3
      4        12        9
           22      6        15
```

9. a £16   b £63
10. £8, £4.20, £3.50, £1.95, 65p

Test A3   page 22

1. a 37   b 10
2. a <   b >
3. 4, 8, **12**, **16**, 20, 24
4. 12, **9**, **6**, 3, 0, **–3**
5. 200.5
6.
```
      8  4  4
  x         6
  ----------
  5  0  6  4
```
7. 1800
8. a 421   b 113
9.

	Even	Not even
less than 20	14, 16, **10**	15, 17, **9**
not less than 20	24, 26, **28**	25, 29, **27**

10. a 8   b 80   c 18

1

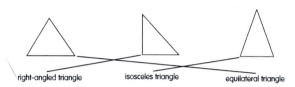

right-angled triangle   isosceles triangle   equilateral triangle

2 check childrens' diagrams

3 a

b 4 right angles

4 B

5 C

6

7

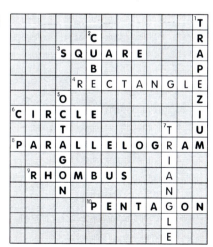

I drew a square based pyramid   I drew a cuboid   I drew a cone   I drew a sphere

Jake   Mai   Khalid   Hannah

8 D

9

10

										¹T
		²C								R
	³S	Q	U	A	R	E				A
		B								P
		⁴R	E	C	T	A	N	G	L	E
	⁵O									Z
⁶C	I	R	C	L	E					I
	T						⁷T			U
⁸P	A	R	A	L	L	E	L	O	G	R	A	M
	G							I		
⁹R	H	O	M	B	U	S		A		
	N						N		
			¹⁰P	E	N	T	A	G	O	N
							L	
							E	

[1 mark for each pair of correct answers]

1 isosceles

2 a rhombus **b** equal sides/diagonals cross at 90°

3 square-based pyramid

4 C

5 A and E

6 B and D

7

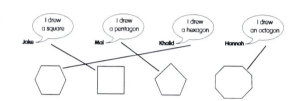

I drew a square   I drew a pentagon   I drew a hexagon   I drew an octagon

Jake   Mai   Khalid   Hannah

8 a cuboid **b** triangular prism

9 A and F

10

1 any pairs of integers that sum to 17

2 equilateral

3 kite

4 triangular prism

5 D

6 A and B

7 C and K

8 A and D

9 B and D

10

Test C1 page 38

1. **a** 1000 ml

2. **a** 2000 **b** 1.75

3. **a** 1000 **b** 0.7

4. 400 g

5. 29 cm

6. 10

7. Vertical axis: 2, 4, 6, 8
   Horizontal axis: red, green, blue, yellow

8. **a** Jake **b** Mai

9. **a** 20p **b** 40p

10. Mai

Test C2 page 40

1. **a** 1000 **b** 500

2. **a** 2000 **b** 0.175

3. **a** 1500 **b** 0.07

4. 2 m

5. 1000 g

6. £260

7.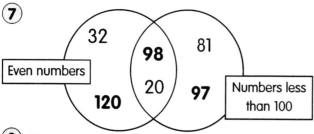

8. 55

9. **a** 60 **b** 15 **c** 15

10. How far do you travel to school?
    How did you come to school today? Or equivalent.

Test C3 page 42

1. 250

2. **a** 3500 **b** 25

3. **a** 250 **b** 0.05

4. 2 km

5. 500 ml

6. 225 g

7. **a** 50 **b** 75

8. **a** Mai **b** 2 worms

9. **a** £12,000 **b** £5000

10. Hannah

Test D1
page 48

(1) 11:58 *10:58*

(2) B

(3) 360°

(4) A

(5) 10 cm²

(6) C8

(7) 175 g

(8) **a** 13 coins **b** £7.60

(9) **a** 35 minutes
   b 10 minutes
   c 1 hour (or 60 minutes)

(10) **a** Post Office **b** 2 miles **c** south

Test D2
page 50

(1) A2, C2 and D2

(2) G4

(3) D

(4) B

(5) 180°

(6) C

(7) **a** 4 **b** 16

(8) **a** £1.10 b 90p

(9) **a** 2.5 hours or $2\frac{1}{2}$ hours **b** 40 minutes

(10) **a** School **b** 3 miles **c** north

Test D3
page 52

(1) **a** 0.56 m **b** 125 m

(2) C1, C2 and C4

(3) J8

(4) C

(5) 9 cm²

(6) C

(7) horizontal

(8) **a** 10 cm **b** 8 cm

(9) **a** 20 cm **b** 16 cm²

(10) **a** school **b** 5 miles **c** north-east

Test E1 — page 58

1. **a** 50   **b** 75
2. **a** false   **b** true
3. **a** true   **b** true
4. $\frac{1}{3}$
5. $\frac{1}{2} = \frac{6}{12} = \frac{10}{20} = \frac{9}{18}$
6. **a** 3   **b** 5
7. $32 - 7$
8. 39, 78
9. **a** >   **b** <
10. B and D

Test E2 — page 60

1. 10
2. 8
3. **a** 100   **b** 150
4. $\frac{3}{4}, 1\frac{1}{2}, 2$
5. **a** <   **b** >
6. $\frac{1}{4} = \frac{6}{24} = \frac{5}{20} = \frac{9}{36}$
7.
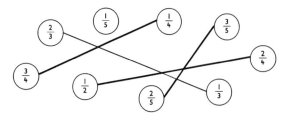
8. 12
9. C
10. **a** 32 children   **b** 24 boys

Test E3 — page 62

1. 370
2. **a** 56   **b** 4.8
3. **a** 40, 5   **b** 63, 7
4. $\frac{3}{4} = \frac{6}{8} = \frac{15}{20} = \frac{9}{12}$
5. **a** £1.20   **b** 40p
6. 6
7. **a** 21   **b** 8
8. Hannah
9. $\frac{1}{4}$
10. **a** 24 children   **b** 8 girls

Measuring Success in Maths: Year 4 Class Record Sheet – Mental Maths Tests

GL assessment
the measure of potential

Name of School _____

Teacher _____   Class _____

First name	Last name	A1 Raw score (/15)	A2 Raw score (/15)	A3 Raw score (/15)	B1 Raw score (/15)	B2 Raw score (/15)	B3 Raw score (/15)	C1 Raw score (/15)	C2 Raw score (/15)	C3 Raw score (/15)	D1 Raw score (/15)	D2 Raw score (/15)	D3 Raw score (/15)	E1 Raw score (/15)	E2 Raw score (/15)	E3 Raw score (/15)
	Date of test:															

Measuring Success in Maths: Year 4 Class Record Sheet – Written Tests

Name of School _____

Teacher _____

Class _____

GL assessment
the measure of potential

First name	Last name	A1 Raw score (/15)	A2 Raw score (/15)	A3 Raw score (/15)	B1 Raw score (/15)	B2 Raw score (/15)	B3 Raw score (/15)	C1 Raw score (/15)	C2 Raw score (/15)	C3 Raw score (/15)	D1 Raw score (/15)	D2 Raw score (/15)	D3 Raw score (/15)	E1 Raw score (/15)	E2 Raw score (/15)	E3 Raw score (/15)
	Date of test:															